SIMPLE SONGS FOR BANJO

40 EASY SONGS TO PLAY ON 5-STRING BANJO

ARRANGED BY
FRED SOKOLOW

EDITORIAL ASSISTANCE BY
RONNY SCHIFF

T0083319

2	Introduction		46	The Night They Drove Old Dixie Down
3	Clawhammer and the Basic Strum		48	Old Man
4	Ballad of Jed Clampett		51	Puff the Magic Dragon
6	Blue Moon of Kentucky		54	(Ghost) Riders in the Sky (A Cowboy Legend)
8	Clinch Mountain Backstep		57	Ripple
10	Cold Rain and Snow		60	Rocky Top
12	East Bound and Down		66	Roll in My Sweet Baby's Arms
14	Folsom Prison Blues		68	Salty Dog Blues
16	Freight Train		70	Shady Grove
20	Friend of the Devil		63	Sweet Baby James
22	Gentle on My Mind		72	Teach Your Children
17	Ho Hey		76	This Land Is Your Land
24	I Am a Man of Constant Sorrow		75	Tom Dooley
26	I Saw the Light		78	Wagon Wheel
32	I Walk the Line		81	Wayfaring Stranger
34	If It Hadn't Been for Love		94	The Weight
29	Jambalaya (On the Bayou)		84	Where Have All the Flowers Gone?
36	Keep on the Sunny Side		86	Wildwood Flower
39	The Last Thing on My Mind		88	Will the Circle Be Unbroken
42	The Long Black Veil		90	You Are My Sunshine
44	Mama Tried		92	Your Cheatin' Heart

ISBN 978-1-70515-040-5

Visit Hal Leonard Online at
www.halleonard.com

World headquarters, contact:
Hal Leonard
7777 West Bluemound Road
Milwaukee, WI 53213
Email: info@halleonard.com

In Europe, contact:
Hal Leonard Europe Limited
1 Red Place
London, W1K 6PL
Email: info@halleonardeurope.com

In Australia, contact:
Hal Leonard Australia Pty. Ltd.
4 Lentara Court
Cheltenham, Victoria, 3192 Australia
Email: info@halleonard.com.au

INTRODUCTION

This collection of tunes is for beginning banjo players, or for intermediate players who want to expand their repertoire. Many of the songs are bluegrass standards ("Salty Dog," "Roll in My Sweet Baby's Arms," "I Am a Man of Constant Sorrow"), and a banjo is usually played whenever they are performed or recorded. Other songs are country standards like "Jambalaya (on the Bayou)" and "Mama Tried" that are well suited to the 5-string, even though it wasn't included on their original recordings. There are also pop songs like "Wagon Wheel" by Old Crow Medicine Show and Neil Young's "Old Man," whose first recordings actually featured banjo. Plus, you'll also find folk songs like "This Land Is Your Land" and "Tom Dooley" that countless banjo players have performed and recorded over the years.

The songs are arranged three different ways:

> Some have the melody line written in music notation, plus lyrics and chord grids, so you can strum the banjo and sing the songs.

> Some have all that, plus the melody of the song written in tablature.

> Some include a banjo arrangement, so you can play the melody with a basic strum or clawhammer style.

A few tunes have capo instructions to get you playing in the same key as the original recording of the song, so you can play along with Glen Campbell (and his banjo player, John Hartford, who wrote the song) on "Gentle on My Mind." That usually involves raising the pitch of the 5th string, so there are instructions for that as well: for example, some songs will say: "Capo 2, 5th string to A," which means "Place the capo at the 2nd fret and tune the 5th string up to A."

There are many musical genres represented here, and the banjo sounds great with all of them!

Good luck and good picking!

Fred Sokolow

P.S.: When a song has capo instructions, the chords written above the music are "in respect to the capo." For example, if the song is in the key of A and the instructions are "Capo 2, 5th String to A," the arrangement shows an open-string (unfretted) chord as G. Because of the capo, it will sound like A, but it plays like a G chord.

CLAWHAMMER AND THE BASIC STRUM

To play the songs that are arranged as banjo instrumentals, like "I Am a Man of Constant Sorrow" or "Wildwood Flower," you need to know the *basic strum* or the *clawhammer strum*. You can play the arrangements with either technique.

The Basic Strum

Play all the melody notes by picking up with your index finger. Whenever there's a pause in the melody, fill in the gap with this three-part basic strum, that has a *boom-chick-a* rhythm:

Boom: Pick up on any string with your index finger (on the flesh, not the nail).

Chick: Brush down on the 1st, 2nd and 3rd strings with the back nail of your middle- or ring finger.

-A: Pick down on the 5th string with your thumb.

Practice this bar, over and over:

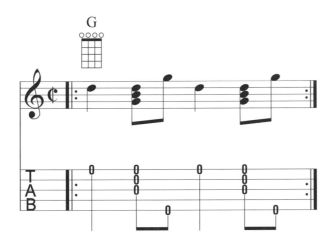

The Clawhammer Style:

This very old banjo strum is just like the basic strum, except the "*boom*" is played with a downward stroke of the index or middle finger's nail, instead of an up-stroke. The "*chick*" downstroke can be played with the fingernail of the index, middle or ring finger, whichever comes naturally to you.

Ballad of Jed Clampett

from the Television Series THE BEVERLY HILLBILLIES

Words and Music by Paul Henning

Key of A
Capo 2, 5th String to A

Verse
Moderately fast

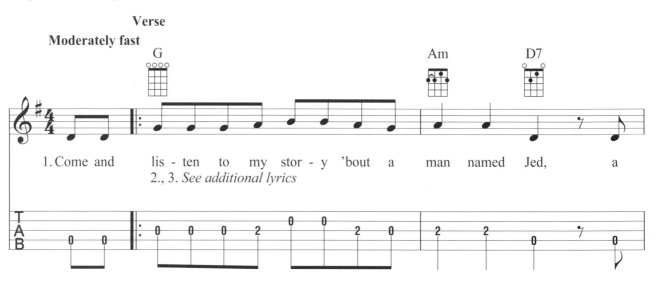

1. Come and lis-ten to my stor-y 'bout a man named Jed, a
2., 3. *See additional lyrics*

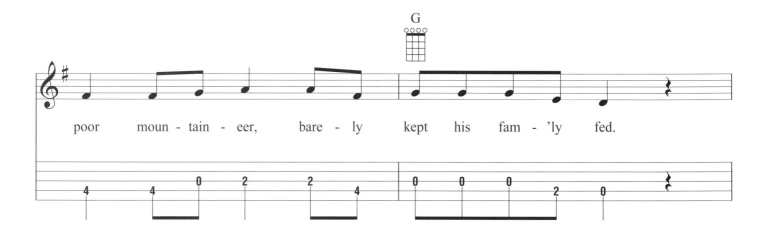

poor moun-tain-eer, bare-ly kept his fam-'ly fed.

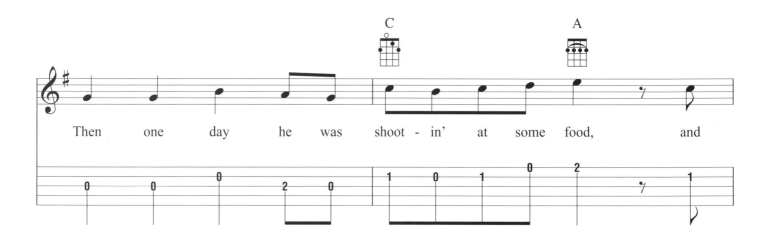

Then one day he was shoot-in' at some food, and

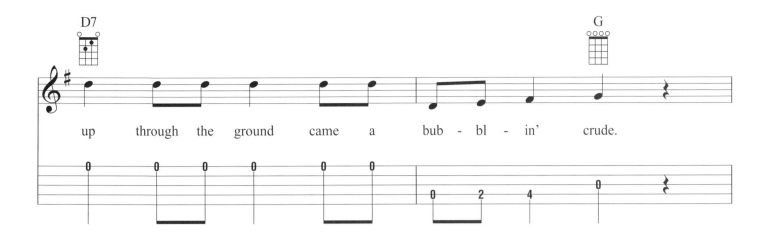

up through the ground came a bub - bl - in' crude.

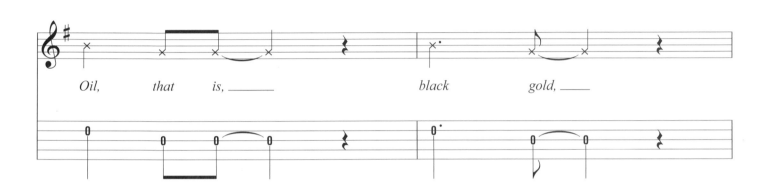

Oil,   that   is, _____   black   gold, _____

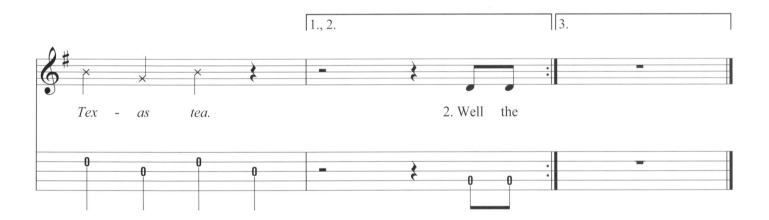

|1., 2.| |3.|

Tex - as tea.   2. Well the

Additional Lyrics

2. Well, the first thing you know, old Jed's a millionaire.
   The kin folks said, "Jed, move away from there."
   Said California was the place he ought to be,
   So they loaded up the truck and they moved to Beverly.
   Hills, that is, swimming pools, movie stars.

3. Well, now it's time to say goodbye to Jed and all his kin.
   They would like to thank you folks for kindly dropping in.
   You're all invited back next week to this locality,
   To have a heaping helping of their hospitality.
   Hillbilly, that is. Set a spell, take your shoes off. Y'all come back now, hear?

Blue Moon of Kentucky

Words and Music by Bill Monroe

Key of B♭

Capo 3, 5th String to B♭

Verse

Slow

1. Blue moon of ___ Ken-tuck-y, keep on shin-ing, shine

on the one that's gone and proved ___ un-true. Blue

moon of ___ Ken-tuck-y, keep on shin-ing, shine

on the one who's gone and left ___ me blue. It was

Clinch Mountain Backstep

Words and Music by Ralph Stanley and Carter Stanley

Key of A
Capo 2, 5th String to A

Moderately

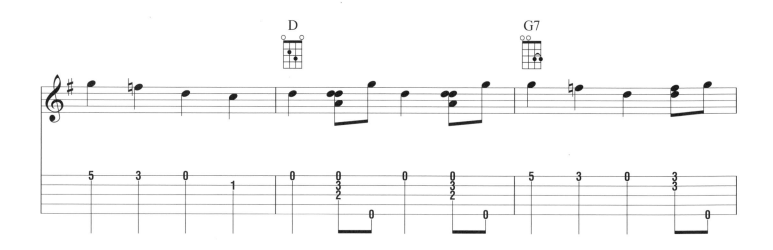

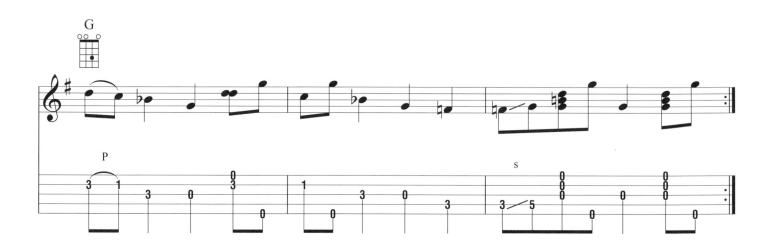

Cold Rain and Snow

Words and Music by Jerry Garcia, Phil Lesh, Ronald McKernan, Bob Weir and William Kreutzmann

Additional Lyrics

2. She came walking down the stairs,
   Combin' her long yellow hair,
   Her cheeks lookin' pretty as a rose.
   As a rose, her cheeks lookin' pretty as a rose.

3. I've done all that I can do.
   Trying to get along with you
   And I ain't gonna be treated this-a way,
   This-a way, no I ain't gonna be treated this-a way.

East Bound and Down

from the Universal Film SMOKEY AND THE BANDIT
Words and Music by Jerry Reed and Dick Feller

Verse

1. Keep your foot hard on the ped - al, son,
2. *See additional lyrics*

nev - er mind __ them brakes. Let it all hang out, 'cause

we've got a run __ to make. The boys are

thirs - ty in At - lan - ta, and there's beer in Tex - ar -

kan - a, and we'll bring it back, no mat - ter what __ it

D.C. al Coda   ⊕ **Coda**

takes.

Additional Lyrics

2. Ol' Smokey's got them ears on and he's hot on your trail.
   He ain't gonna rest 'til you're in jail.
   So you got to dodge 'im and you got to duck 'im,
   You got to keep that diesel truckin'.
   Just put that hammer down and give it hell.

Folsom Prison Blues

Words and Music by John R. Cash

Key of G

Verse

Moderately

1. I hear the train a - com - in', it's roll - in' 'round the bend,
2., 3., 4. *See additional lyrics*

_ and I ain't seen the sun - shine since

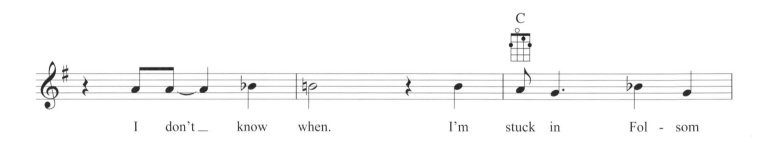

I don't _ know when. I'm stuck in Fol - som

Pris - on, and time keeps dra - gin'

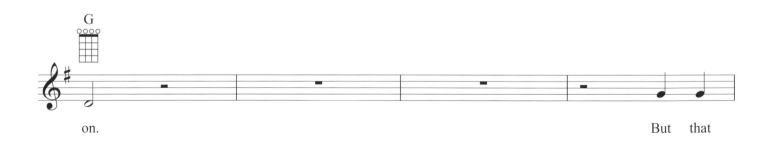

on. But that

train   keeps   a   -   roll   -   in',   on   down   to

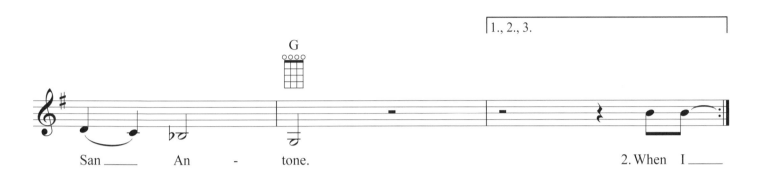

San _____   An   -   tone.   2. When   I _____

Additional Lyrics

2. When I was just a baby, my mama told me, "Son,
   Always be a good boy, don't ever play with guns."
   But I shot a man in Reno, just to watch him die.
   When I hear that whistle blowin,' I hang my head and cry.

3. I bet there's rich folk eatin' from a fancy dinin' car.
   They're prob'ly drinkin' coffee and smokin' big cigars.
   Well I know I had it comin', I know I can't be free.
   But those people keep a-movin', and that's what tortures me.

4. Well, if they freed me from this prison, if that railroad train was mine,
   I bet I'd move it on a little farther down the line.
   Far from Folsom Prison, that's where I want to stay.
   And I'd let that lonesome whistle blow my blues away.

Freight Train

Words and Music by Elizabeth Cotten

1. Freight train, freight train, run so fast, ___ freight train,
2., 3. *See additional lyrics*

freight train, run so fast. ___ Please don't tell what

train I'm on, so they won't know what route I'm going.

Additional Lyrics

2. When I'm dead and in my grave,
   No more good times here I crave.
   Place the stones at my head and feet
   And tell them all that I've gone to sleep.

3. When I die, Lord, bury me deep,
   Way down on old Chestnut Street,
   So I can hear old Number Nine
   As she comes rolling by.

Ho Hey

Words and Music by Jeremy Fraites and Wesley Schultz

Key of C
Intro
Moderately

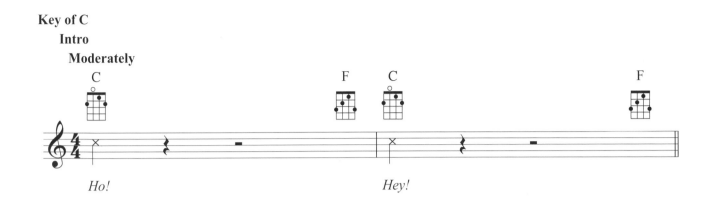

Ho!　　　　　　　　　　　　　Hey!

1. *Ho!* I've been try'n to do ___ it right. ___
2., 3. *See additional lyrics*

Hey! I've been liv-in' a lone - ly life. ___

Ho! I've been sleep - in' here ___ in-stead.

Hey! I've been sleep - in' in ___ my bed. ___

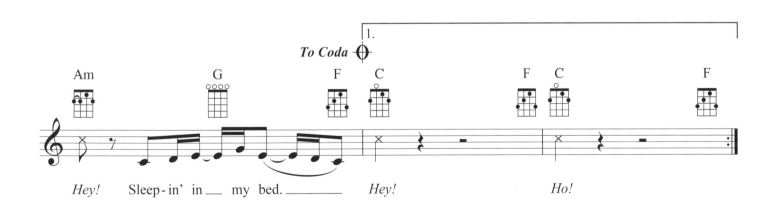

Hey! Sleep-in' in ___ my bed. ___

Hey!

Ho!

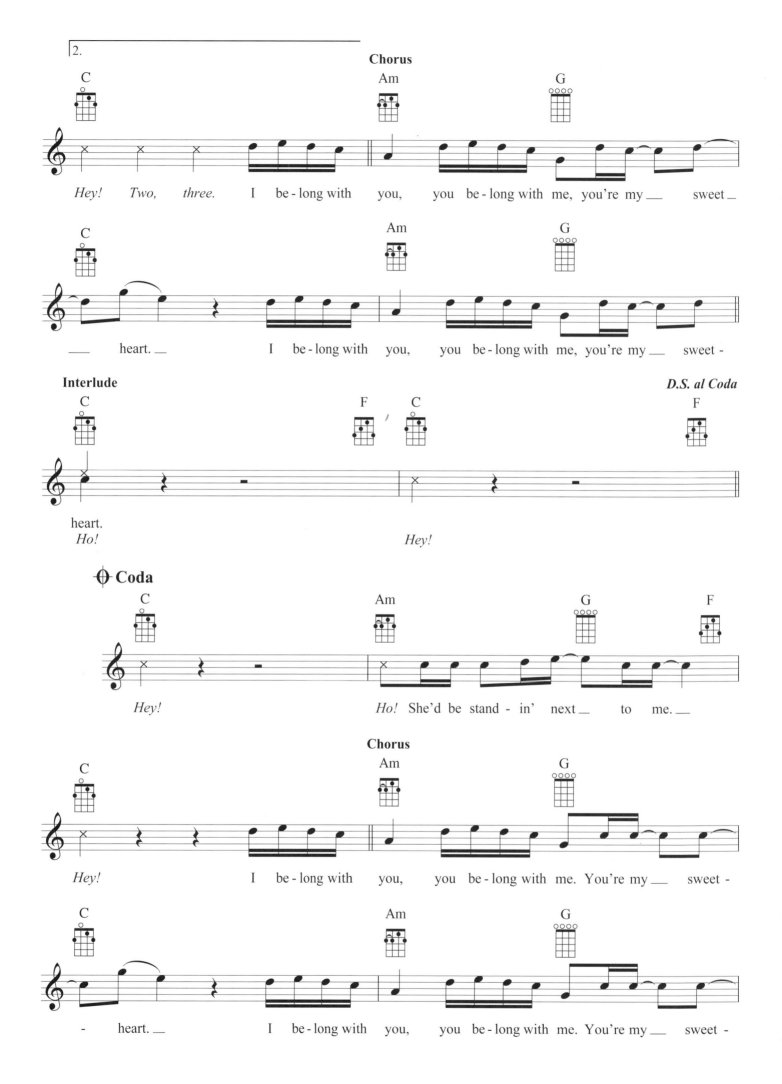

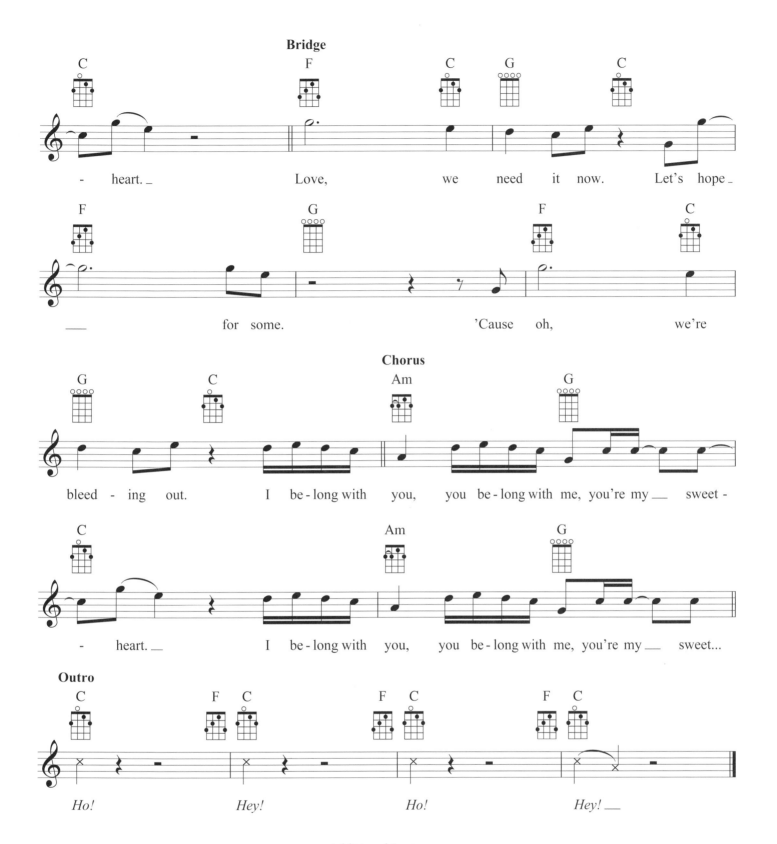

Additional Lyrics

2. *Ho!* So show me family,
   Hey! all the blood that I will bleed.
   Ho! I don't know where I belong,
   Hey! I don't know where I went wrong.
   Ho! But I can write a song. *Hey!*

3. *Ho!* I don't think you're right for him.
   Hey! Look at what it might've been
   Ho! if you took a bus to Chinatown,
   Hey! I'd be standing on Canal
   Ho! and Bowery. *Hey!*

Friend of the Devil

Words by Robert Hunter
Music by Jerry Garcia and John Dawson

𝄋 **Bridge**

Got two rea-sons why I cry a - way each lone-ly night. __ The

first one's named Sweet Anne Ma-rie, and she's my heart's de - light. __

Sec-ond one is pri-son, ba - by, the sher-iff's on my trail, and

if he catch-es up with me, __ I'll spend my life in jail.

D.S. al Coda   ⟡ **Coda**

night. _____

Additional Lyrics

2. Ran into the devil, babe, he loaned me twenty bills.
   I spent the night in Utah in a cave up in the hills.
   Set out runnin' but I take my time, a friend of the devil is a friend of mine.
   If I get home before daylight, I just might get some sleep tonight.

3. I ran down to the levee but the devil caught me there.
   He took my twenty dollar bill and vanished in the air.
   Set out runnin' but I take my time, a friend of the devil is a friend of mine.
   If I get home before daylight, I just might get some sleep tonight.

4. Got a wife in Chino, babe, and one in Cherokee.
   The first one says she's got my child but it don't look like me.
   Set out runnin' but I take my time, a friend of the devil is a friend of mine.
   If I get home before daylight, I just might get some sleep tonight

Gentle on My Mind

Words and Music by John Hartford

Additional Lyrics

2. It's not clingin' to the rocks and ivy planted on their columns now that bind me,
   Or something that somebody said because they thought we fit together walkin'.
   It's just knowing that the world will not be cursing or forgiving
   When I walk along some railroad track and find
   That you're movin' on the back roads by the rivers of my memory
   And for hours you're just gentle on my mind.

3. Though the wheat fields and the clothes lines and the junkyards
   And the highways come between us,
   And some other woman's cryin' to her mother 'cause she turned and I was gone,
   I still might run in silence, tears of joy might stain my face
   And the summer sun might burn me till I'm blind,
   But not to where I cannot see you walkin' on the back roads
   By the rivers flowin' gentle on my mind.

4. I dip my cup of soup back from a gurglin' cracklin' cauldron in some train yard
   My beard a rustlin' coal pile and a dirty hat pulled low across my face.
   Through cupped hands 'round a tin can, I pretend to hold you to my breast and find
   That you're waitin' from the back roads
   By the rivers of my memory ever smilin', ever gentle on my mind.

I Am a Man of Constant Sorrow

Words and Music by Carter Stanley and Ralph Stanley

Key of F
5th String at F

Verse
Moderately

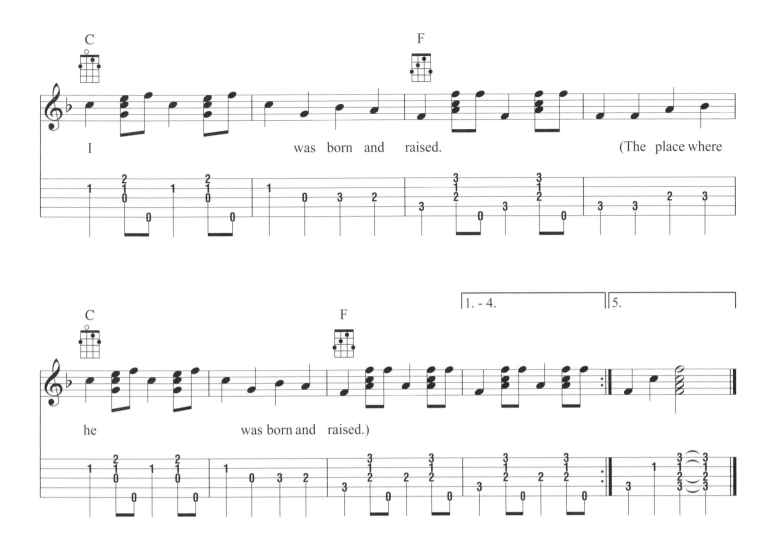

Additional Lyrics

2. For six long years I've been in trouble,
   No pleasure here on earth I find.
   For in this world I'm bound to ramble.
   I have no friends to help me now.
   (He has no friends to help him now.)

3. It's fare thee well, my own true lover.
   I never expect to see you again.
   For I'm bound to ride that northern railroad.
   Perhaps I'll die upon this train.
   (Perhaps he'll die upon this train.)

4. You can bury me in some deep valley,
   For many years where I may lay.
   Then you may learn to love another,
   While I am sleeping in my grave.
   (While he is sleeping in his grave.)

5. Maybe your friends think I'm just a stranger,
   My face you never will see no more.
   But there is one promise that is given:
   I'll meet you on God's golden shore.
   (He'll meet you on God's golden shore.)

I Saw the Light

Words and Music by Hank Williams

Key of G

Verse

Moderately

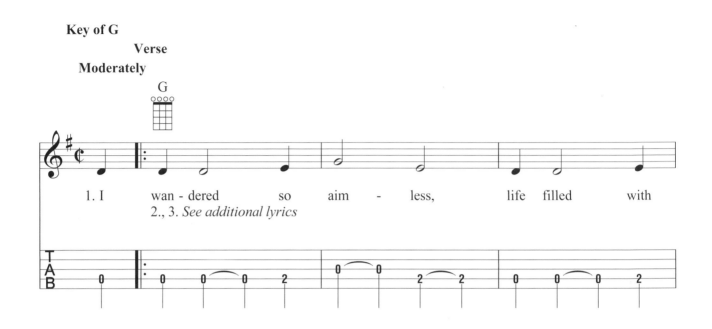

1. I wan - dered so aim - less, life filled with
2., 3. *See additional lyrics*

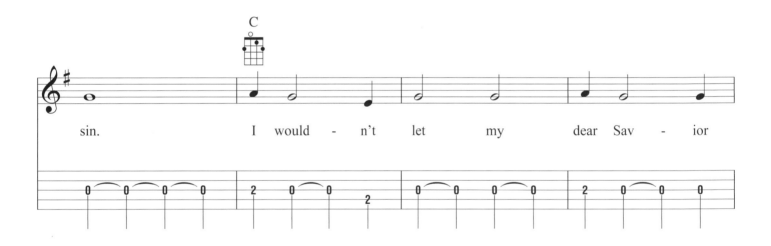

sin. I would - n't let my dear Sav - ior

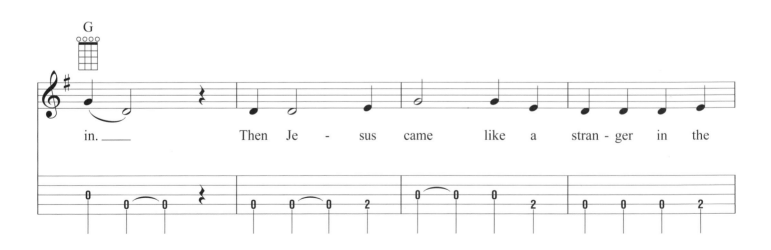

in. ____ Then Je - sus came like a stran - ger in the

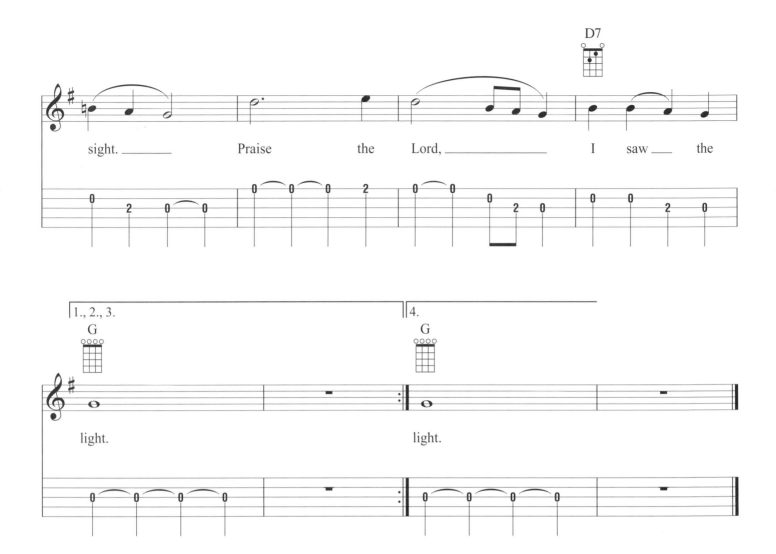

Additional Lyrics

2. Just like a blind man I wandered along.
   Worries and fears, I claimed for my own.
   Then like the blind man that God gave back his sight.
   Praise the Lord, I saw the light.

3. I was a fool to wander and stray.
   For straight is the gate and narrow the way.
   Now I have traded the wrong for the right.
   Praise the Lord, I saw the light.

Jambalaya
(On the Bayou)

Words and Music by Hank Williams

Key of G

Verse

Moderately

gun, we'll have big fun on the ba - you.

Chorus

Jam - ba - lay'__ and a craw - fish pie and a fi - lé

gum - bo, 'cause to - night I'm gon - na

see my ma chaz - a mi - o. Pick gui -

30

Additional Lyrics

2. The Thibodeaux, the Fontaineaux, the place is buzzin'.
   Kinfolk come to see Yvonne by the dozen.
   Dress in style, and go hog wild, me oh, my oh.
   Son of a gun, we'll have big fun on the bayou.

3. Settle down far from town, get me a pirogue,
   And I'll catch all the fish in the bayou.
   Swap my mon' to buy Yvonne what she need-o.
   Son of a gun, we'll have big fun on the bayou.

I Walk the Line

Words and Music by John R. Cash

Key of G

Moderately

Verse

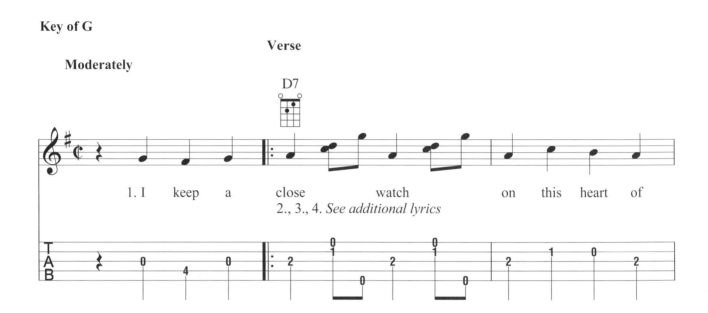

1. I keep a close watch on this heart of
2., 3., 4. *See additional lyrics*

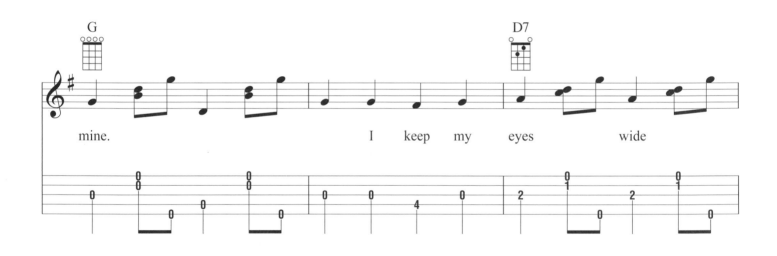

mine. I keep my eyes wide

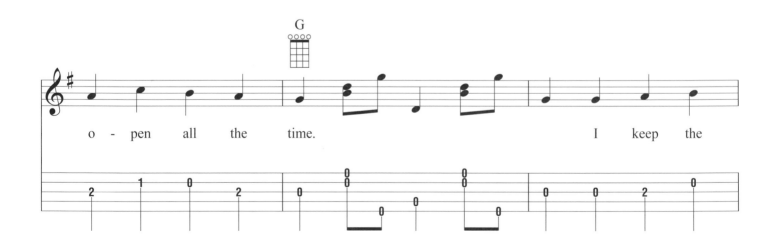

o - pen all the time. I keep the

Additional Lyrics

2. I find it very, very easy to be true.
   I find myself alone when each day is through.
   Yes, I'll admit that I'm a fool for you.
   Because you're mine, I walk the line.

3. As sure as night is dark and day is light,
   I keep you on my mind both day and night,
   And happiness I've known proves that I'm right.
   Because you're mine, I walk the line.

4. You've got a way to keep me on your side.
   You give me cause for love that I can't hide.
   For you, I know I'd even try to turn the tide.
   Because you're mine, I walk the line.

If It Hadn't Been for Love

Words and Music by Michael Henderson and Chris Stapleton

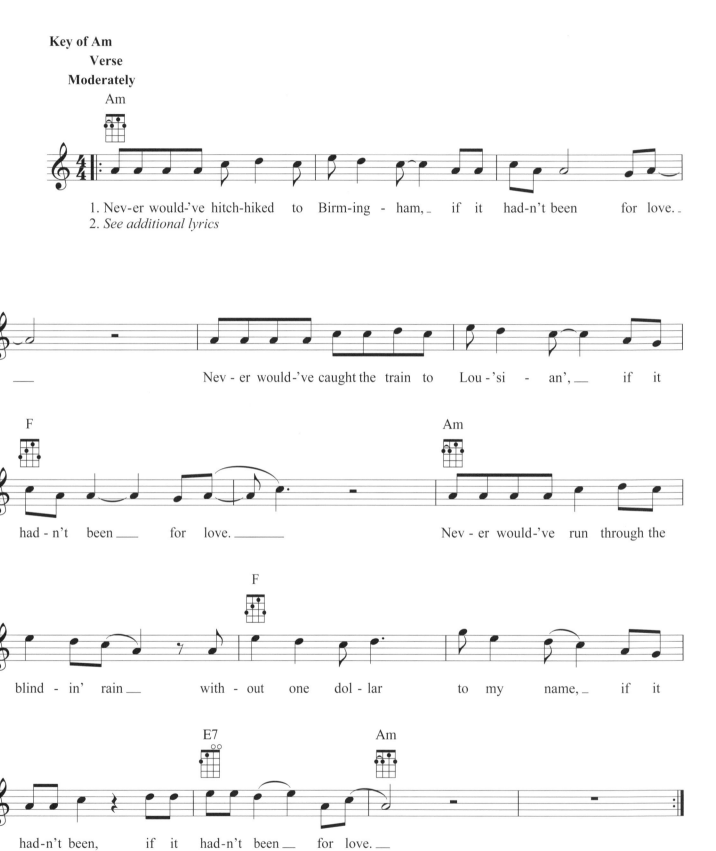

Chorus

Four cold walls ___ a - gainst my will. ___ At least I know ___ she's ly - in' still.

Four cold walls ___ with - out pa - role. ___ Lord have mer - cy on ___ my soul.

Additional Lyrics

2. Never woulda seen the trouble that I'm in, if it hadn't been for love.
Woulda been gone like a wayward wind, if it hadn't been for love.
Nobody knows it better than me, I wouldn't be wishing I was free,
If it hadn't been, if it hadn't been for love.

Keep on the Sunny Side

Words and Music by A.P. Carter

Additional Lyrics

2. Though a storm and its fury break today,
   Crushing hopes that we cherished so dear,
   Clouds and storms will in time pass away,
   The sun again will shine bright and clear.

3. Let us greet with a song of hope each day,
   Though the moment be cloudy or fair.
   Let us trust in our Savior away,
   To keep us, everyone, in His care

The Last Thing on My Mind

Words and Music by Tom Paxton

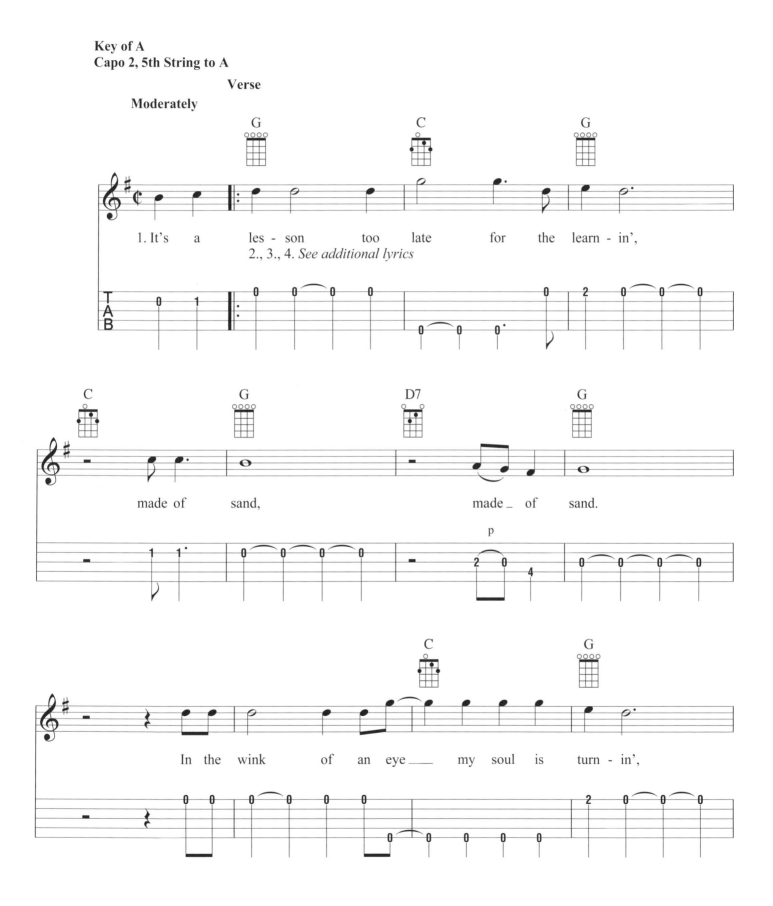

Key of A
Capo 2, 5th String to A

Verse

Moderately

1. It's a les-son too late for the learn-in',
2., 3., 4. *See additional lyrics*

made of sand,   made of sand.

In the wink of an eye____ my soul is turn-in',

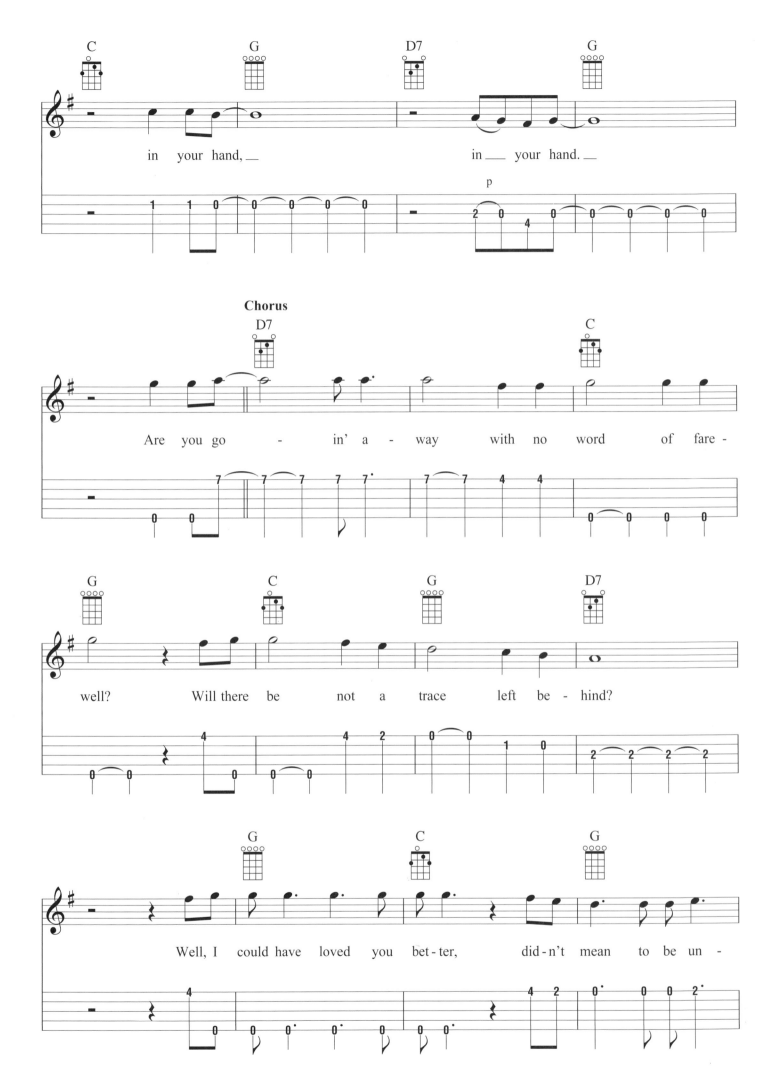

Additional Lyrics

2. You've got reasons a-plenty for goin'.
   This I know, this I know.
   For the weeds have been steadily growin'.
   Please don't go, please don't go.

3. As I lie in my bed in the mornin',
   Without you, without you,
   Every song in my breast dies a bornin',
   without you, without you.

4. As we walk, all my thoughts are a-tumblin'
   'Round and 'round, 'round and 'round.
   Underneath the street the subway's rumblin',
   Underground, underground.

The Long Black Veil

Words and Music by Marijohn Wilkin and Danny Dill

Chorus

walks these hills _ in a long _ black veil. She

vis - its my grave _ when the night winds wail. _____

___ No - bod - y knows, _____ no - bod - y

sees. No - bod - y knows _____ but _____

To Coda ⊕   *D.C. al Coda*   ⊕ **Coda**
             (take 2nd ending)

___ me. _____   3. The

Additional Lyrics

3. The scaffold was high and eternity near.
   She stood in the crowd and shed not a tear.
   But sometimes at night when the cold wind moans,
   In a long black veil, she cries over my bones.

Mama Tried

Words and Music by Merle Haggard

Key of D
Capo 2, 5th String to A

Additional Lyrics

3. Dear old Daddy, rest his soul, left my mom a heavy load.
   She tried so very hard to fill his shoes.
   Working hours without rest, wanted me to have the best.
   She tried to raise me right but I refused.

The Night They Drove Old Dixie Down

Words and Music by Robbie Robertson

Chorus

mem - ber, oh, so well. The night they drove — old Dix - ie down, —

— and the bells — were ring - in', the night they drove —

— old Dix - ie down, — and the peo — ple were sing - in', they went,

"Na, _____ na, na, na, na, na. — Na, na, na, na, na, na, —

1.

2.

— na, na, na." —

Additional Lyrics

2. Back with my wife in Tennessee, when one day she called to me,
"Virgil, quick, come see, there goes Robert E Lee."
Now I don't mind choppin' wood, and I don't care if the money's no good.
Ya take what ya need and ya leave the rest,
But they should never have taken the very best.

3. Like my father before me, I will work the land,
And like my brother above me, who took a Rebel stand.
He was just eighteen, proud and brave, but a Yankee laid him in his grave.
I swear by the blood below my feet,
You can't raise a Caine back up when he's in defeat.

Old Man

Words and Music by Neil Young

Key of D
5th String to A

Chorus
Moderately slow

Old man, look at my life, I'm a lot like you were.

you were.

Verse

1. Old man, look at my life; twen-ty-four and there's so much more.
2. *See additional lyrics*

Live a-lone in a par-a-dise __ that makes one think __ of two. _____

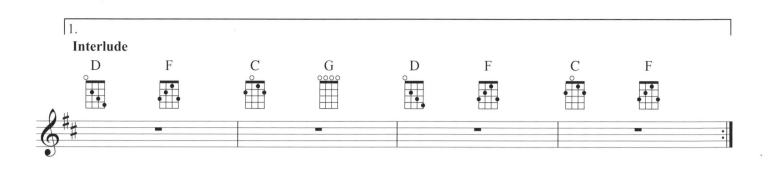

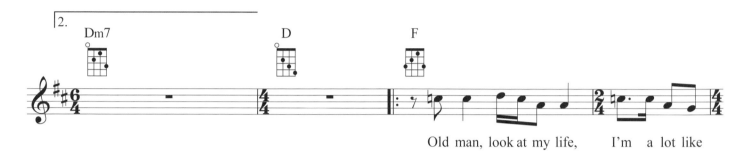

Old man, look at my life,   I'm a lot like

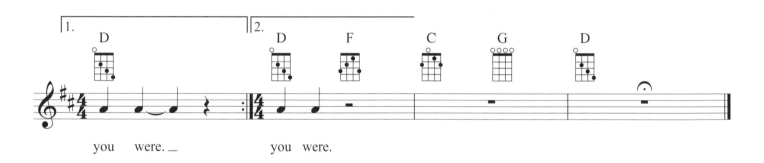

you were. __   you were.

Additional Lyrics

2. Lullabies, look in your eyes, run around the same old town.
   Doesn't mean that much to me to mean that much to you.
   I've been first and last. Look at how the time goes past,
   But I'm all alone at last, rolling home to you.

Puff the Magic Dragon

Words and Music by Lenny Lipton and Peter Yarrow

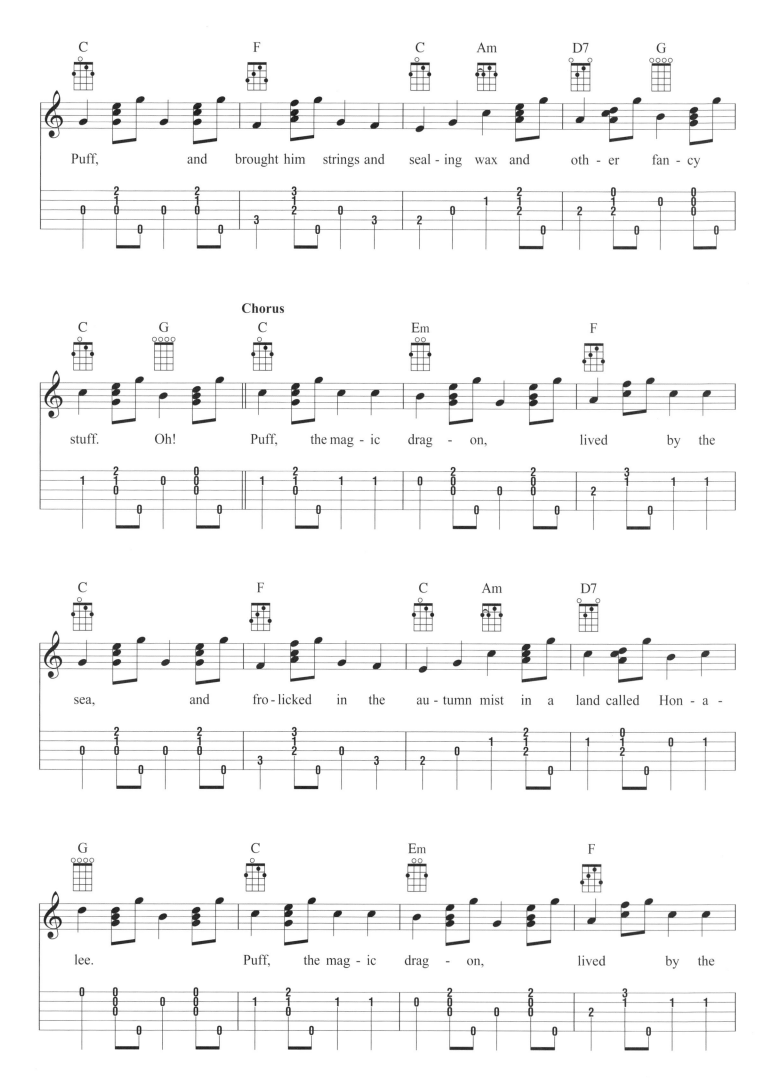

Chorus

Additional Lyrics

2. Together they would travel on a boat with billowed sail.
   Jackie kept a lookout perched on Puff's gigantic tail.
   Noble kings and princes would bow whene'er they came.
   Pirate ships would lower their flags when Puff roared out his name.

3. A dragon lives forever, but not so little boys.
   Painted wings and giant's rings make way for other toys.
   One gray night it happened, Jackie Paper came no more.
   And Puff, that mighty dragon, he ceased his fearless roar.

4. His head was bent in sorrow, green scales fell like rain.
   Puff no longer went to play along the cherry lane.
   Without his lifelong friend, Puff could not be brave.
   So Puff, that mighty dragon, sadly slipped into his cave.

(Ghost) Riders in the Sky

(A Cowboy Legend)

from RIDERS IN THE SKY
By Stan Jones

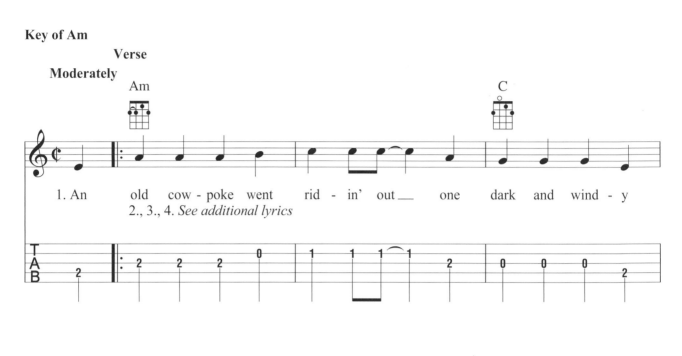

1. An old cow-poke went rid-in' out ___ one dark and wind-y
2., 3., 4. *See additional lyrics*

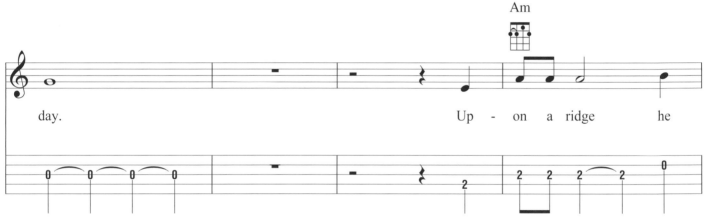

day. Up - on a ridge he

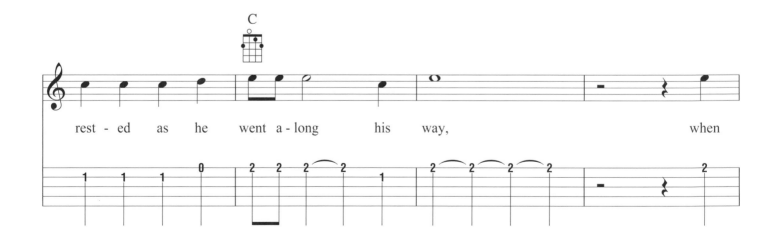

rest-ed as he went a-long his way, when

all at once a might-y herd of red-eyed cows he saw, a-

plow-in' through the rag-ged skies _____ and up a cloud-y

draw. Yip - ee - i -

Chorus

yay, _____ yip-ee-i-

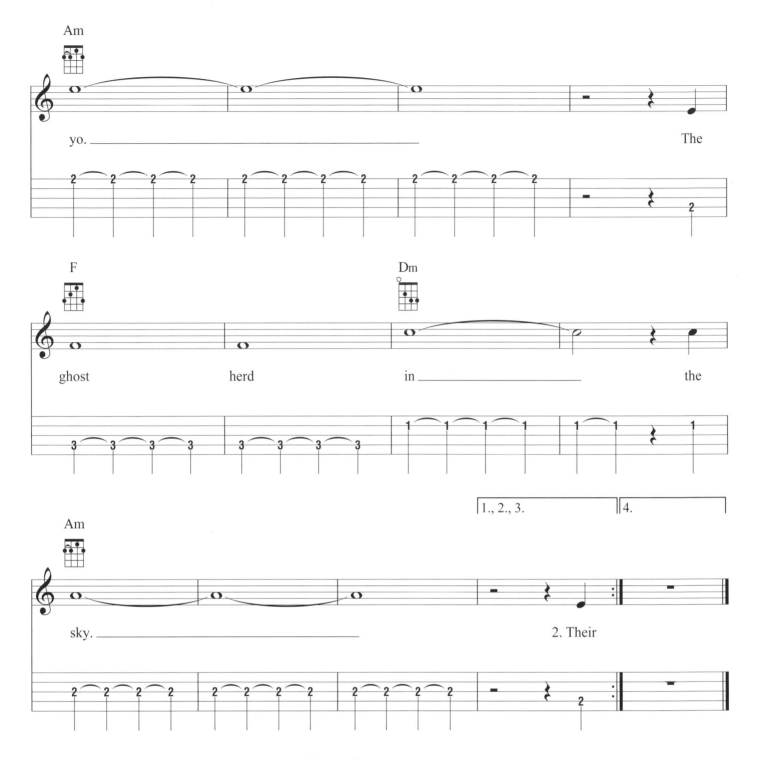

Additional Lyrics

2. Their brands were still on fire and their hooves were made of steel.
   Their horns were black and shiny and their hot breath he could feel.
   A bolt of fear went through him as they thundered through the sky,
   For he saw the riders coming hard and he heard their mournful cry.

3. Their faces gaunt, their eyes were blurred, their shirts all soaked with sweat.
   They're ridin' hard to catch that herd but they ain't caught 'em yet.
   'Cause they've got to ride forever on the range up in the sky,
   On horses snorting fire, as they ride on, hear their cry.

4. As the riders loped on by him, he heard one call his name:
   "If you want to save your soul from hell a-riding on our range,
   Then cowboy change your ways today or with us you will ride,
   Tryin' to catch the devils herd across these endless skies."

Ripple

Words by Robert Hunter
Music by Jerry Garcia

Key of G

Moderately

Chorus

Am · · · · · · · · · · · D7 · · · · · · · · · · · ·

Rip - ple in ___ still wa - ter. ___ when there

G · · · · · · · C · · · · · · · A · · · · · · · D7 · · · · · · · ·

is no peb - ble tossed, nor wind to ___ blow. 3. Reach out ___ your
5. You who _

Verse

G · · · · · · · · · · · · · · · C · · · · · · · · · · · · · ·

hand, if your cup _ be emp - ty. If your cup _
choose to lead _ must fol - low, but _ if _

G ·

___ is full, may it be a - gain. Let it ___ be
___ you fall, you _ fall a - lone. If you _ should

C ·

known: there is ___ a foun - tain _
stand, then who's _ to guide you? _

To Coda ⊕   *D.S. al Coda*
                     (take 2nd ending)

G · · · · · · · D7 · · · · · · · C · · · · · · · G · · · · · · · ·

that was not _ made by the hands _ of men. ___ 4. There is a road, _
If I knew the _ way, I would take _ you home. _

Additional Lyrics

4. There is a road, no simple highway,
   Between the dawn and the dark of night,
   And if you go no one may follow.
   That path is for your steps alone.

Rocky Top

Words and Music by Boudleaux Bryant and Felice Bryant

Chorus

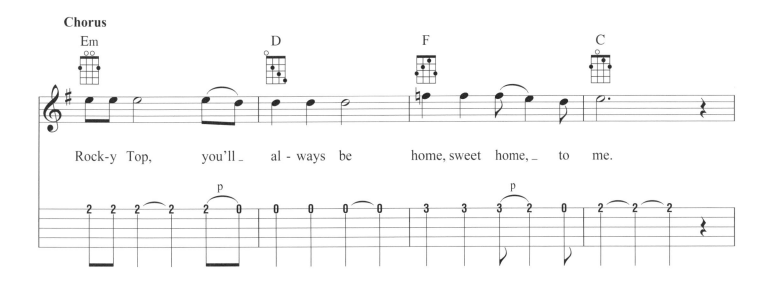

Rock-y Top, you'll _ al - ways be home, sweet home, _ to me.

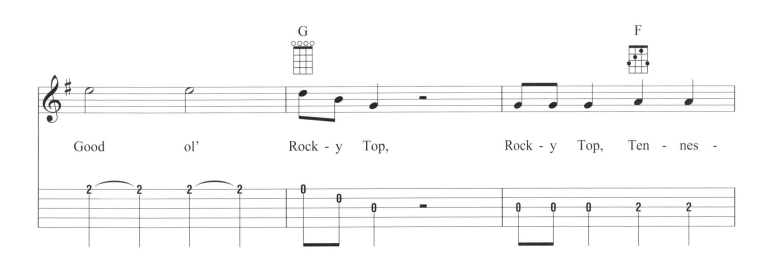

Good ol' Rock - y Top, Rock - y Top, Ten - nes -

To Coda ⊕

1st time, D.S.
(take repeat)
2nd time, D.S. al Coda
(take 5th ending)

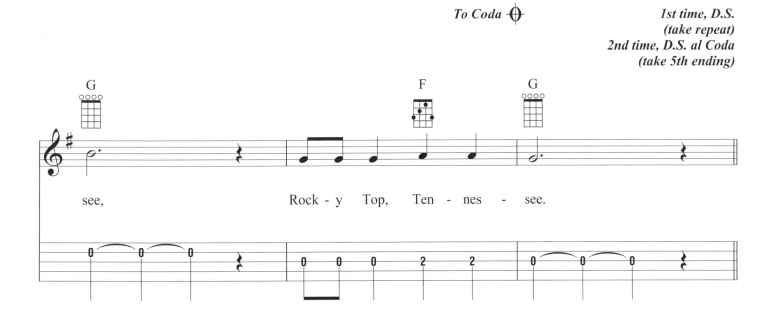

see, Rock - y Top, Ten - nes - see.

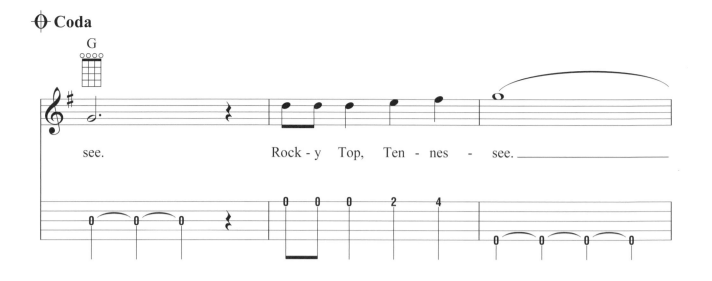

see.   Rock - y Top, Ten - nes - see. _____

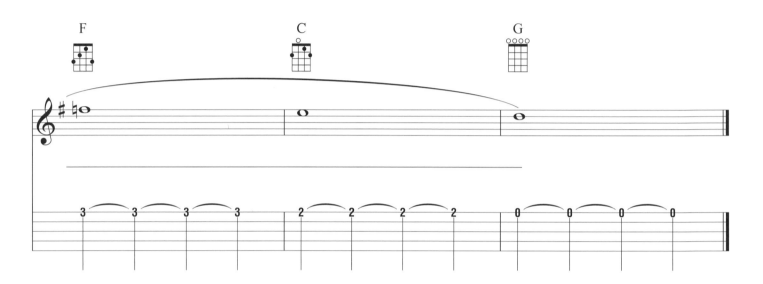

Additional Lyrics

2. Once I had a girl on Rocky Top,
   Half bear the other half cat,
   Wild as a mink but sweet as soda pop.
   I still dream about that.

3. Once two strangers climbed old Rocky Top,
   Looking for a moonshine still.
   Strangers ain't come come down from Rocky Top.
   Reckon they never will.

4. Corn won't grow at all on Rocky Top,
   Dirt's too rocky by far.
   That's why all the folks on Rocky Top
   Get their corn from a jar.

5. I had years of cramped up city life,
   Trapped like a duck in a pen.
   All I know is, it's a pity
   Life can't be simple again.

Sweet Baby James

Words and Music by James Taylor

Key of D
Capo 2, 5th String to A

Verse

Moderately

1. There is a young cow-boy, he lives on the range.
2. *See additional lyrics*

His horse and his cat-tle are his on-ly com-pan-ions.

He works in the sad-dle and he sleeps in the can-yons,

wait-ing for sum-mer, his pas-tures to change. And

Pre-Chorus

as the moon ris - es, he sits by his fire,

think - in' a - bout wom - en and glass - es of beer. And

clos - ing his eyes as the dog - ies re - tire, he

sings out a song ___ which is ___ soft but it's ___ clear, as

if may - be some-one could hear.

Chorus

Good - night, you moon - light la - dies.

Rock - a - bye, ___ sweet Ba - by James. ___

Deep greens and blues ___ are the col - ors I choose. Won't you

let me ___ go down in my ___ dreams? And

rock - a - bye, sweet Ba - by James. 2. Now the

Additional Lyrics

2. Now the first of December was covered with snow.
So was the turnpike from Stockbridge to Boston.
The Berkshires seemed dream-like on account of that frosting,
With ten miles behind me and ten thousand more to go.

Pre-Chorus There's a song that they sing when they take to the highway,
A song that they sing when they take to the sea,
A song that they sing of their home in the sky.
Maybe you can believe it if it helps you to sleep,
But singing works just fine for me.

Roll in My Sweet Baby's Arms

Traditional

Key of G
Verse/Chorus
Fast

1. Ain't gon - na work on the rail - road,
Chorus: Roll in my sweet ba - by's arms,

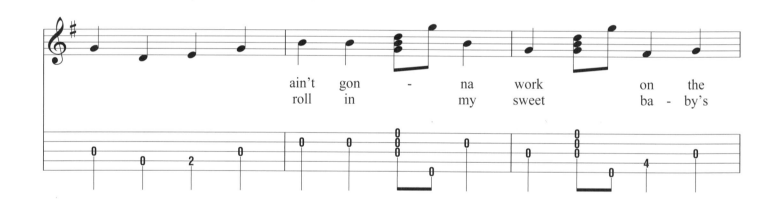

ain't gon - na work on the
roll in my sweet ba - by's

farm.
arms.

Gon - na lay 'round the

Additional Lyrics

2. Now, where was you last Friday night
   While I was lyin' in jail?
   Walkin' the streets with another man,
   You wouldn't even go my bail.

3. I know your parents don't like me,
   They drove me away from your door.
   If I had my life to live over again,
   I'd never go there anymore.

4. Mama's a beauty operator,
   Sister can weave and can spin.
   Dad's got an interest in the old cotton mill,
   Just watch the money roll in.

Salty Dog Blues

Words and Music by Wiley A. Morris and Zeke Morris

Key of G

Verse/Chorus

Fast

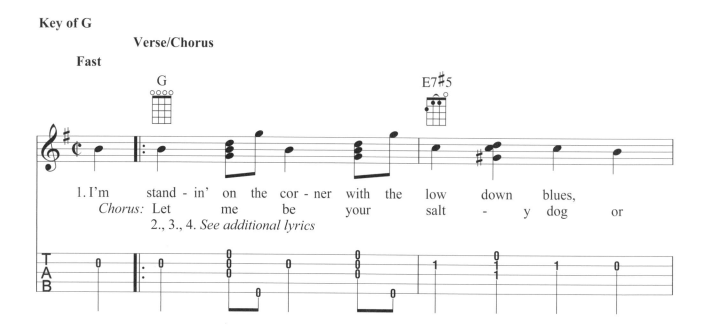

1. I'm stand - in' on the cor - ner with the low down blues,
Chorus: Let me be your low salt - y dog or
2., 3., 4. *See additional lyrics*

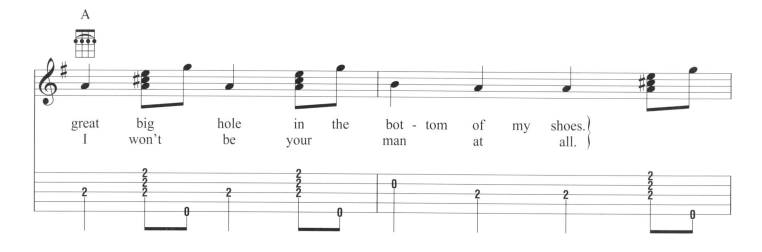

great big hole in the bot - tom of my shoes.
I won't be your man at all.

Hon - ey, let me be your salt - y

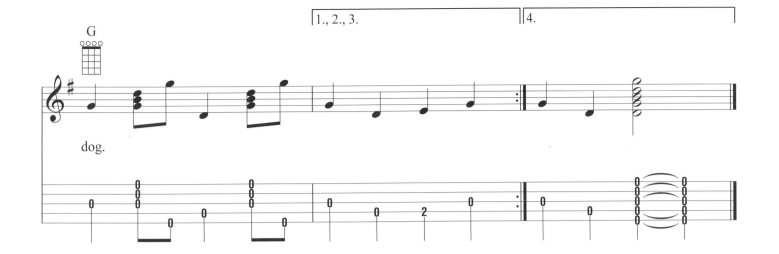

dog.

Additional Lyrics

2. Now look-a here, Sal, I know you,
   A rundown stockin' and a worn-out shoe,
   Honey, let me be your salty dog.

3. I was down in the wildwood settin' on a log,
   Finger on the trigger and an eye on the hog.
   Honey, let me be your salty dog.

4. I pulled the trigger and the gun said "Go,"
   Shot fell over in Mexico.
   Honey, let me be your salty dog.

Shady Grove

Appalachian Folk Song

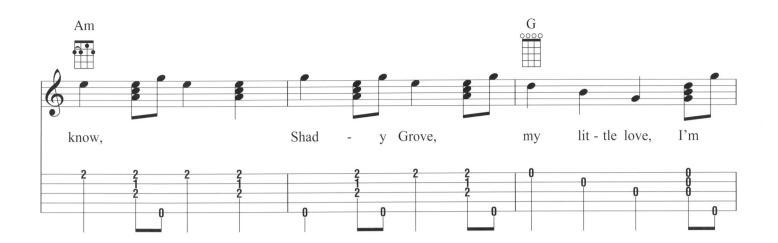

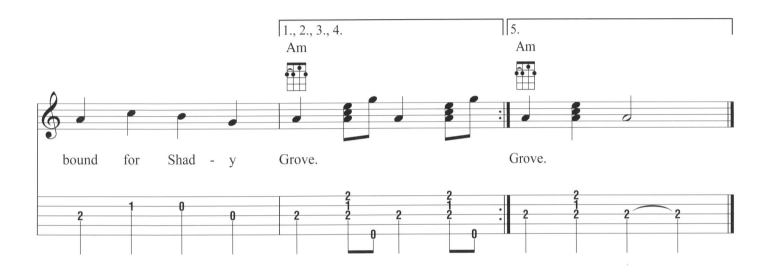

Additional Lyrics

2. Cheeks as red as a blooming rose,
   Eyes of deepest brown,
   You are the darling of my heart,
   Stay 'til the sun goes down.

3. I wish I had a big fine horse
   And corn to feed him on,
   Pretty little girl to stay at home
   And feed him while I'm gone.

4. Wish I had a needle and thread,
   Fine as I could sew.
   I'd sew that pretty girl to my side
   And down the road I'd go.

5. Peaches in the summertime,
   Apples in the fall.
   If I can't have my Shady Grove
   I won't have none at all.

Teach Your Children

Words and Music by Graham Nash

Key of D
Capo 2, 5th String to A

Verse
Moderately

1. You,   who are on   the road, __   must have a
2. Teach   your chil - dren well. __   Their fa-ther's
3., 4. *See additional lyrics*

code __   that __ you can   live by,   and
hell   did __ slow-ly   go by,   and

so,   be - come __ your - self,   be - cause __ the past __
feed   them on ___ your __ dreams.   The one ___ they pick's __

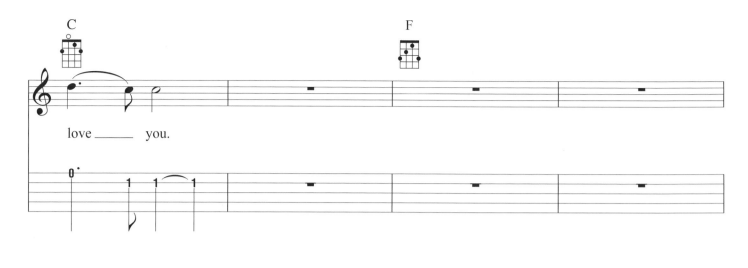

love _____ you.

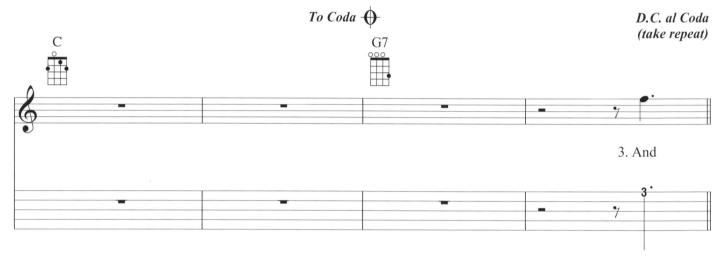

To Coda ✛

D.C. al Coda
(take repeat)

3. And

✛ **Coda**

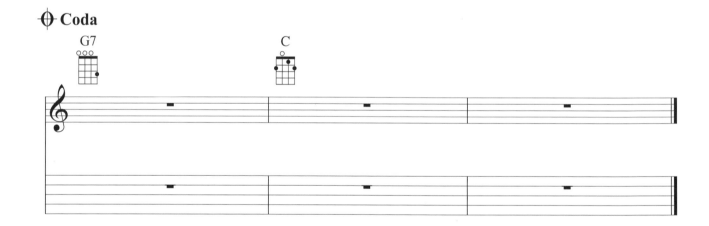

Additional Lyrics

2. And you of tender years,
   Can't know the fears that your elders grew by,
   And so, please help them with your youth.
   They seek the truth before they can die.

4. Teach your parents well.
   Their children's hell will slowly go by.
   And feed them on your dreams.
   The one they pick's the one you'll know by.

Tom Dooley

Words and Music Collected, Adapted and Arranged by Frank Warner, John A. Lomax and Alan Lomax
From the singing of Frank Proffitt

Key of E
Capo 4, 5th String to B

Chorus/Verse
Moderately

Chorus: Hang down your head, Tom Doo - ley, hang down your head and
met her on the moun - tain, there I took her
2., 3. *See additional lyrics*

cry.
life.

Hang down your head, Tom Doo - ley,
Met her on the moun - tain,

1. - 6.
poor boy, you're bound to die.
stabbed her with my knife.

7.
1. I die.
(Repeat Chorus)

Additional Lyrics

2. This time tomorrow, reckon where I'll be,
   Hadn't-a been for Grayson, I'd-a been in Tennessee.

3. This time tomorrow, reckon where I'll be,
   Down in some lonesome valley hangin' from a white oak tree.

This Land Is Your Land

Words and Music by Woody Guthrie

Key of C

Verse

Moderately

1. This land is your land, this land is
2. - 5. *See additional lyrics*

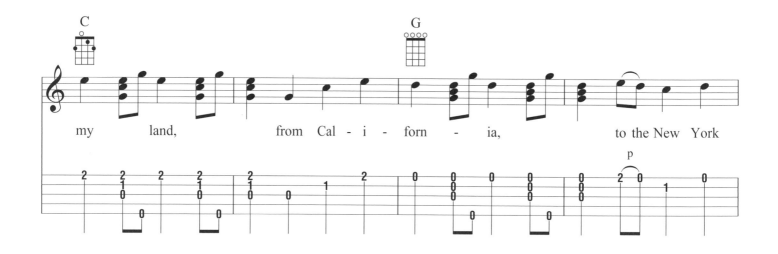

my land, from Cal - i - forn - ia, to the New York

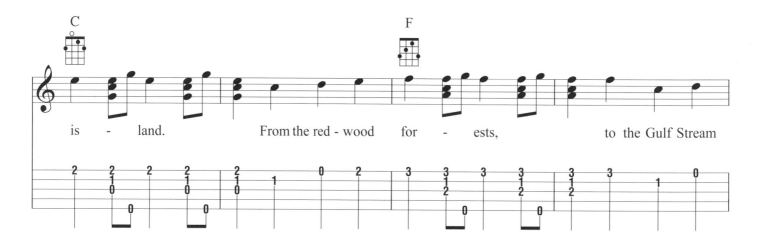

is - land. From the red - wood for - ests, to the Gulf Stream

wa - ters, this land was

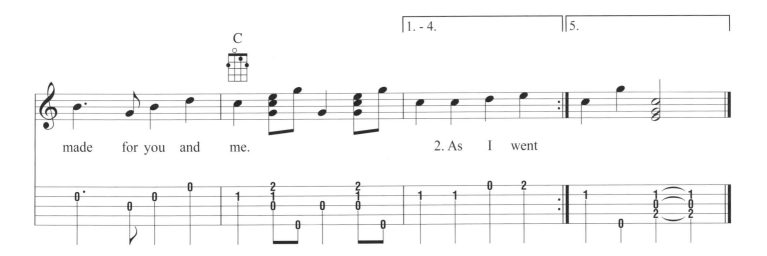

made for you and me. 2. As I went

Additional Lyrics

2. As I went walking that ribbon of highway,
   I saw above me that endless skyway.
   I saw below me that golden valley.
   This land was made for you and me.

3. I've roamed and rambled and I followed my footsteps
   To the sparkling sands of her diamond deserts.
   And all around me a voice was sounding:
   "This land was made for you and me."

4. When the sun came shining, and I was strolling,
   And the wheat fields waving and the dust clouds rolling,
   As the fog was lifting, a voice was chanting:
   "This land was made for you and me."

5. As I went walking I saw a sign there,
   And on the sign it said "No Trespassing."
   But on the other side it didn't say nothing.
   That side was made for you and me.

Wagon Wheel

Words and Music by Bob Dylan and Ketch Secor

Key of A
Capo 2, 5th String up to A

Verse
Moderately

Additional Lyrics

2. Runnin' from the cold up in New England,
   I was born to be a fiddler in an old time string band.
   My baby plays a guitar, I pick a banjo now.
   Oh, north country winters keep a-getting me down.
   I lost my money playing poker so I had to leave town,
   But I ain't turning back to living that old life no more.

3. Walkin' to the south out of Roanoke,
   I caught a trucker out of Philly, had a nice long toke,
   But he's a heading west from the Cumberland gap to Johnson City, Tennessee.
   And I gotta get a move on before the sun.
   I hear my baby calling my name and I know that she's the only one,
   And if I die in Raleigh, at least I will die free.

Wayfaring Stranger

Southern American Folk Hymn

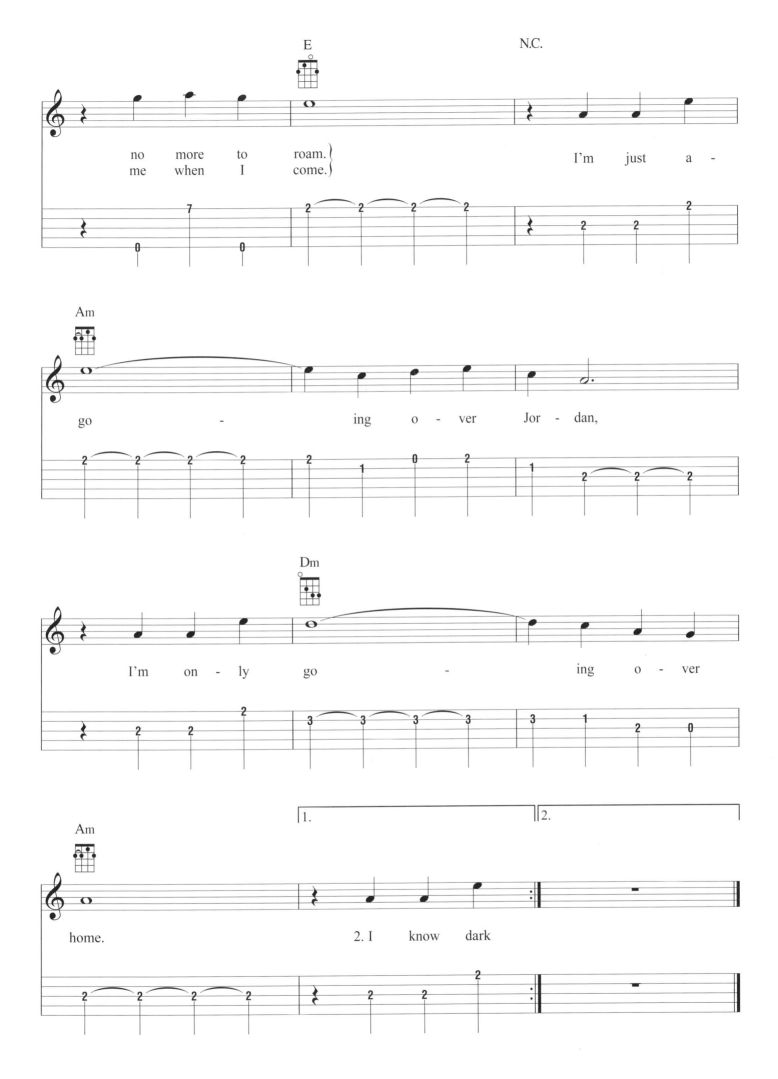

Where Have All the Flowers Gone?

Words and Music by Pete Seeger

Key of B♭

Capo 3, 5th String to B♭

Verse

Moderately

1. Where have all the flow-ers gone, long time pass - ing? Where have all the flow-ers gone, long time a - go? Where have all the

2. - 5. *See additional lyrics*

Additional Lyrics

2. Where have all the young girls gone, long time passing?
   Where have all the young girls gone, long time ago?
   Where have all the young girls gone? Gone to young men, every one.
   When will they ever learn? When will they ever learn?

3. Where have all the young men gone, long time passing?
   Where have all the young men gone, long time ago?
   Where have all the young men gone? Gone for soldiers, every one.
   When will they ever learn? When will they ever learn?

4. Where have all the soldiers gone, long time passing?
   Where have all the soldiers gone, long time ago?
   Where have all the soldiers gone? Gone to graveyards, every one.
   When will they ever learn? When will they ever learn?

5. Where have all the graveyards gone, long time passing?
   Where have all the graveyards gone, long time ago?
   Where have all the graveyards gone? Gone to flowers, every one.
   When will they ever learn? When will they ever learn?

Wildwood Flower

Words and Music by A.P. Carter

Key of G

Verse

Moderately

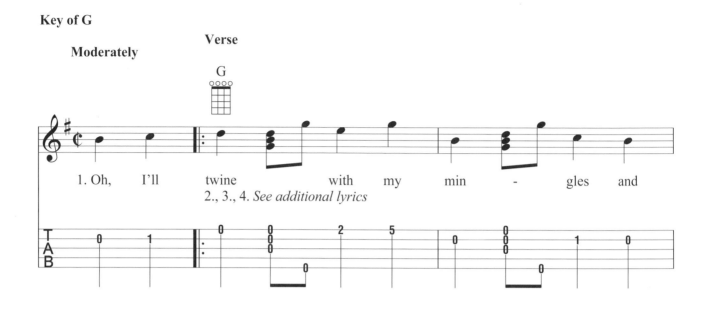

1. Oh, I'll twine with my min - gles and
2., 3., 4. *See additional lyrics*

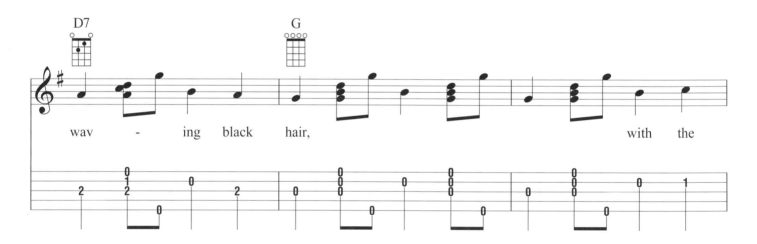

wav - ing black hair, with the

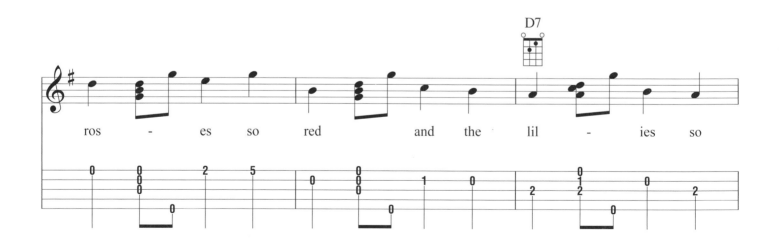

ros - es so red and the lil - ies so

Additional Lyrics

2. I will dance, I will sing and my laugh shall be gay.
   I will charm every heart, in his crown I will sway.
   When I woke from my dreaming, my idols was clay.
   All portion of love had all flown away.

3. Oh, he taught me to love him and promised to love,
   And to cherish me over all others above.
   Oh my heart is now wondering, no misery can tell.
   He left with no warning, no word of farewell.

4. He taught me to love him and called me his flower
   That was blooming to cheer him through life's dreary hour.
   I long to see him and regret the dark hour
   He's gone and neglected this pale wildwood flower.

Will the Circle Be Unbroken

Words by Ada R. Habershon
Music by Charles H. Gabriel

Key of G

Verse/Chorus

Moderately

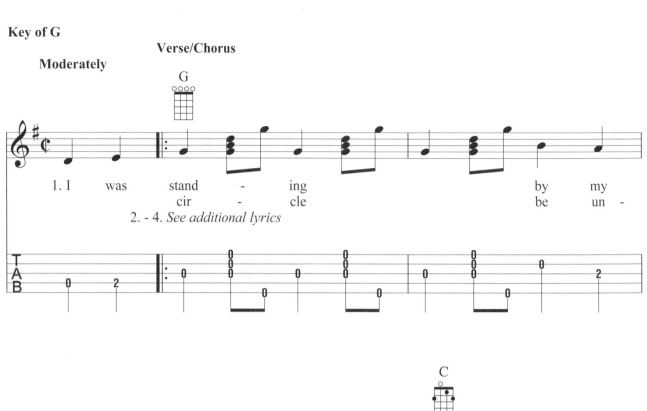

1. I was stand - ing by my
cir - cle be un -
2. - 4. *See additional lyrics*

win - dow, on a cold and
bro - ken, bye and bye, Lord,

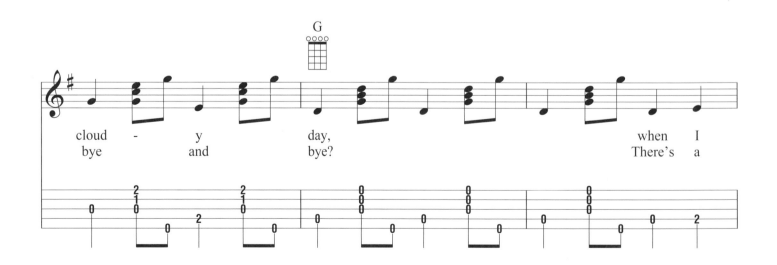

cloud - y day, when I
bye and bye? There's a

Additional Lyrics

2. Lord, I told the undertaker, "Undertaker, please drive slow,
   For this body you are hauling, Lord, I hate to see her go."

3. I followed close behind her, tried to hold up and be brave.
   But I could not hide my sorrow when they laid her in the grave.

4. Went back home, Lord, my home was lonesome, since my mother, she was gone.
   All my brothers, sisters cryin', what a home so sad and 'lone.

You Are My Sunshine

Words and Music by Jimmie Davis

Capo 5, 5th String to C

Moderately

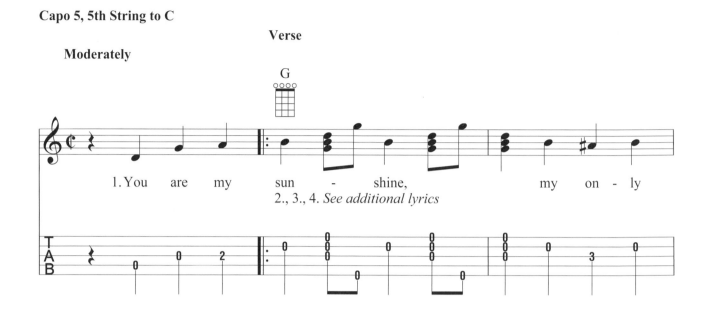

1. You are my sun - shine, my on - ly
2., 3., 4. *See additional lyrics*

sun - shine. You make me hap - py

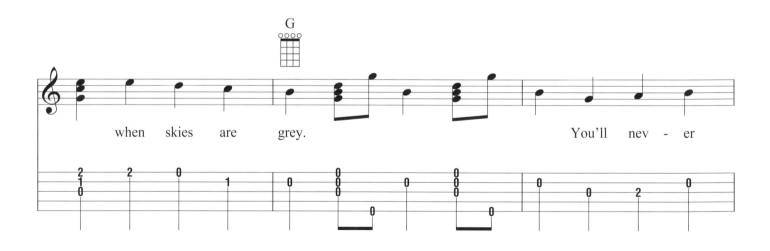

when skies are grey. You'll nev - er

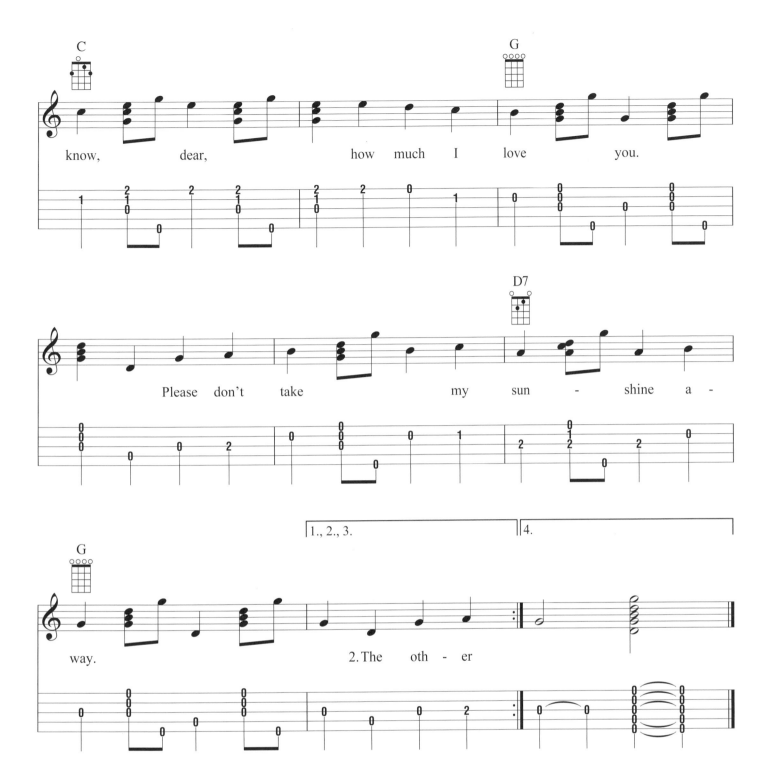

Additional Lyrics

2. The other night dear, as I lay sleeping,
   I dreamed I held you in my arms.
   When I awoke, dear, I was mistaken,
   And I hung my head and cried.

3. I'll always love you and make you happy,
   If you will only say the same.
   But if you leave me to love another,
   You'll regret it all some day.

4. You told me once dear, you really loved me
   And no one else dear, could come between
   But now you've left me and love another.
   You have shattered all my dreams.

Your Cheatin' Heart

Words and Music by Hank Williams

The Weight

By Jaime Robbie Robertson

and, and you put the load, (you put the load) right on

me. ———

Additional Lyrics

2. I picked up my bag, I went lookin' for a place to hide,
   When I saw Carmen and the Devil walkin' side by side.
   I said, "Hey, Carmen, come on let's go downtown."
   She said, "I gotta go but my friend can stick around."

3. Go down, Miss Moses, there's nothin' you can say.
   It's just ol' Luke and Luke's waitin' on the Judgment Day.
   "Well, Luke, my friend, what about young Anna Lee?"
   He said, "Do me a favor, son, won't you stay and keep Anna Lee company?"

4. Crazy Chester followed me and he caught me in the fog.
   He said, "I will fix your rack if you'll take Jack, my dog."
   I said, "Wait a minute, Chester, you know I'm a peaceful man."
   He said, "That's okay, boy, won't you feed him when you can."

5. Catch a Cannon Ball now to take me down the line.
   My bag is sinkin' low and I do believe it's time
   To get back to Miss Fanny, you know she's the only one
   Who sent me here with her regards for everyone.